To Andrew
with love from
Dad
Christmas 1991

CHARING CROSS
TO ORPINGTON

Vic Mitchell and Keith Smith

First published November 1991

ISBN 0 906520 96 7

Design and laser typesetting -
Deborah Goodridge
Barbara Mitchell

Published by Middleton Press
Easebourne Lane
Midhurst
West Sussex
Tel: (0730) 813169

Printed & bound by Biddles Ltd,
Guildford and Kings Lynn

CONTENTS

ACKNOWLEDGEMENTS

We have received much assistance from many of the photographers mentioned in the captions and for this we are extremely grateful. Our gratitude also goes to R.Carpenter, R.M.Casserley, Dr.E.Course, C.Hall, J.R.W.Kirkby, N. Langridge, A.Ll.Lambert, Revd.H.Mace, A.C.Mott, J.S.Petley, R.Randell, D.Salter, N.Sprinks, G.T.V.Stacey, E.Staff, N.Stanyon, C.Wilson and our ever supportive wives.

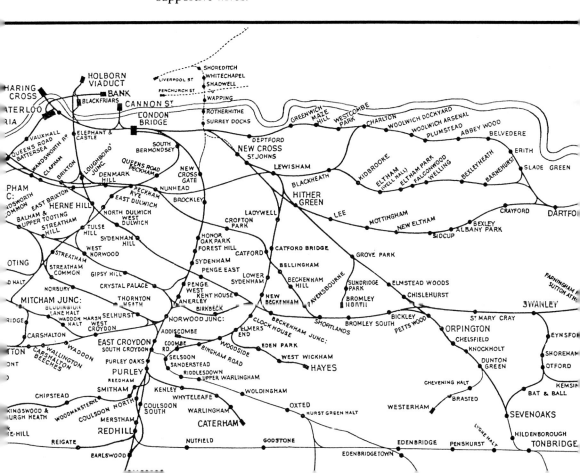

GEOGRAPHICAL SETTING

Near Lewisham, the route leaves the Thames Valley and rises onto London Clay as far as Grove Park. The Bromley North branch and the main line to Orpington traverse the sand and pebbles of the Blackheath Beds, although an outcrop of Chalk is crossed in the vicinity of Elmstead Woods.

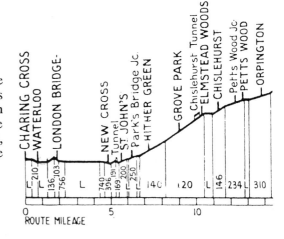

HISTORICAL BACKGROUND

The first passenger line south of the Thames in the London area was the London & Greenwich Railway, which opened between Spa Road and Deptford on 8th February 1836. It was extended to London Bridge on 14th December of that year, the entire route being laid on brick arches.

The South Eastern Railway was forced by Parliament to run its trains from Dover to London Bridge over the tracks of the London & Brighton, the London & Croydon and the London & Greenwich companies. In 1845, it leased the latter which enabled it to develop its North Kent line. This branched south from the L&GR and ran through Lewisham, Black-heath, Woolwich and Dartford to Rochester (Strood), opening on 30th July 1849.

Lines south from Lewisham were opened to Beckenham (on 1st January 1857) and to Chislehurst (on 1st July 1865). A more direct route to Dartford branched from the latter on 1st August 1866, running via Sidcup and becoming known as the "Dartford Loop". The main line was extended from Chislehurst to Sevenoaks on 3rd March 1868, and on to Tonbridge on 1st May of that year. Meanwhile at the London end, the SER had extended (at very great expense) to Charing Cross on 11th January 1864 and into the City at Cannon Street on 1st September 1866. A connection between the Charing Cross line and the London, Chatham & Dover Railway's line through Blackfriars to the City was opened on 1st June 1878.

The locally inspired Bromley Direct Railway was opened as a branch from Grove Park on 1st January 1878. It gave a slightly more direct route to the City than that provided by the LCDR from what was later known as Bromley South. The branch to Bromley (North) was absorbed by the SER on 21st July 1879.

From 1899, the rival SER and LCDR were operated as one by a managing committee and soon became known as the South Eastern & Chatham Railway. Improvements soon followed. Quadrupling of the tracks from the Lewisham area to Orpington commenced in 1900 and connections between the two main lines in the Bickley/Chislehurst district were made in 1902-04.

The route came under the control of the new Southern Railway in 1923. Electrification of the Victoria-Orpington service took place on 12th July 1925, the Charing Cross-Orpington and Bromley North routes following on 28th February 1926.

Nationalisation in 1948 resulted in the formation of British Railways. Following unsuccessful trials with a doubledeck train, peak-hour electric trains were extended to ten coaches from 17th June 1956.

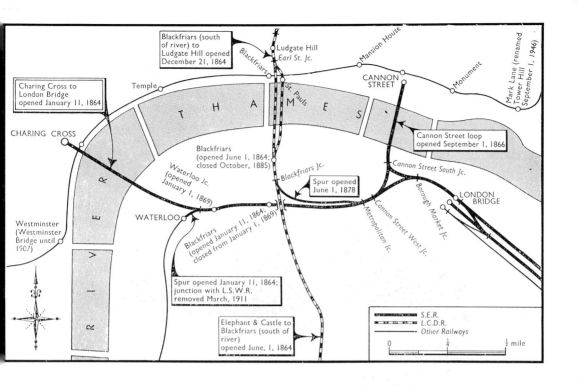

PASSENGER SERVICES

Main Line

Only trains calling at Chislehurst and/or Orpington are considered under this heading, the inner London services being included in other albums.

The table below indicates the number of down trains calling at the stations, their relative importance being seen to change over the sample years.

	Chislehurst		Orpington	
	Weekdays	Sundays	Weekdays	Sundays
1869	9	1	4	1
1890	19	4	15	4
1906	26	14	24	14
1924	21	11	25	12

Electrification resulted in a vastly improved service of two stopping trains per hour, plus one fast hourly between London Bridge and Orpington, on weekdays. The 1936 timetable still showed three trains in most hours but wartime economies resulted in only the Sunday service being reduced initially. Since the mid-1940s the route has had a basic 30 minute interval stopping service, with regular hourly fast trains to Orpington being a feature of the Kent Coast electrification timetable.

Bromley North Branch.

The weekday down trains numbered 26 initially, this quickly being reduced to 20. This increased to 27 in 1906 and 36 in 1910, and was reduced to 28 in 1917 due to WWI but was restored to 30 in 1921 and 37 in 1924.

Electrification in 1926 brought an average weekday service of 53 trains with a basic timetable of two trains per hour, which has been maintained almost without a break ever since, although it was cut to hourly during WWII and restored in 1948. Through working to London has been progressively reduced. It ceased on Sundays in 1958, on Saturdays in 1973 and in off-peak hours on weekdays in May 1976, when a 20-minute interval shuttle service to Grove Park was introduced. In May 1991, all through workings were withdrawn, the off-peak half-hourly service being worked by a 2EPB, with two separate 4EPBs running in the peak hours.

CHARING CROSS

1. The station was constructed on the site of the 1835 Hungerford Market and opened on 11th January 1864. The associated bridge was one of five built across the River Thames in the London area in the 1860s, a period of great railway expansion in the Metropolis. The Charing Cross Railway Co. had been incorporated in 1859 and was largely financed by the SER. In the foreground is the tunnel approach for empty cabs. (Lens of Sutton)

2. The bridge was built on the site of the Hungerford & Lambeth suspension footbridge, which was designed by I.K. Brunel, opened in 1845 and subsequently reused at Clifton near Bristol. Work on the new 7000 ton iron bridge started in 1860 and provision was made for footways on both sides of the bridge. The upstream one was closed in 1887 but the other is still in use, known as Hungerford, after the founder of the first market site on the north bank in 1680. The pedestrian toll generated £4000 per annum initially. (Westinghouse Signals Ltd / Revd.W. Awdry coll.)

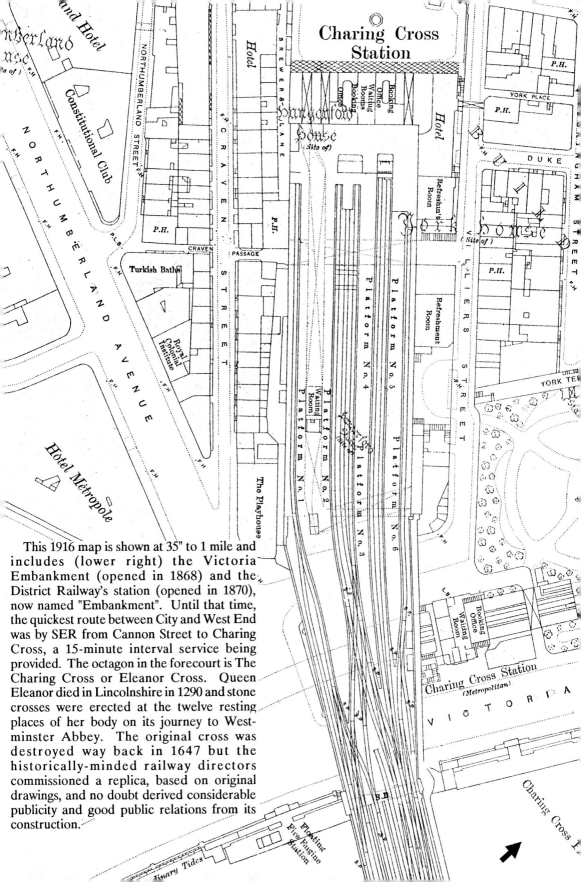

Charing Cross Station

This 1916 map is shown at 35" to 1 mile and includes (lower right) the Victoria Embankment (opened in 1868) and the District Railway's station (opened in 1870), now named "Embankment". Until that time, the quickest route between City and West End was by SER from Cannon Street to Charing Cross, a 15-minute interval service being provided. The octagon in the forecourt is The Charing Cross or Eleanor Cross. Queen Eleanor died in Lincolnshire in 1290 and stone crosses were erected at the twelve resting places of her body on its journey to Westminster Abbey. The original cross was destroyed way back in 1647 but the historically-minded railway directors commissioned a replica, based on original drawings, and no doubt derived considerable publicity and good public relations from its construction.

3. As at most London termini, the railway company built a prestigious hotel. This was opened in 1865 and contained "a rising room, fitted with comfortable seats, in which visitors may be conveyed up or down if they feel indisposed to use the staircases". The hotel had almost 300 rooms and was used by travellers to and from the continent until all boat trains to the Kent Coast were centred on Victoria in 1920. The Eleanor Cross is left of centre. (National Railway Museum).

4. This is the scene after the east end of the roof collapsed on 5th December 1905, killing two workmen and three staff in the adjacent theatre (see map). One of the tie-rods failed and progressive collapse ensued, which gave sufficient time to evacuate passengers and to stop incoming trains. The entire roof was removed and the station reopened on 19th March 1906. Note the mixture of gas and electric lighting, also the signal attached to a lamp post. (British Rail)

5. The roof was rebuilt with lattice girders and iron columns. Electric lighting was pioneered on 10th January 1881 - Liverpool Street was the only other terminus to have such illumination at that time. The SER and the Taff Vale were the first railways to offer a public telegraph service - the office is on the right. (National Railway Museum)

6. The three tracks on the left ran onto the younger part of the bridge, which was added in the mid 1880s. The layout seen here was substantially revised in 1925, ready for electric services. The older bridge was rebuilt in 1979,

the other having been extensively repaired in 1948. The crest was a feature retained, it being replaced in 1985 by a durable one made from self-coloured polyester resin. (National Railway Museum)

7. A 1937 photograph gives good detail of the roof structure. This was damaged by bombing during WWII, as was the upstream side of the bridge. In 1988 a £130m scheme was started which provided a nine storey office block *hanging* from nine 36m wide bowstring trusses, which in turn are supported from columns passing up through the station, each square box column being made from 50mm thick steel plate and carrying 3500 tons. £5.3m was spent on new station offices and information equipment to serve the 120,000 passengers using the station on weekdays. (National Railway Museum)

APPROACH TO WATERLOO EAST

9. Viewed from the offices above Waterloo Station on 13th September 1962, the 11.40 to Hastings has just left Charing Cross, visible in the background. The lion to the left of the main entrance earlier adorned the Lion Brewery, marked on the map as being adjacent to the railway. The brick structure left of centre once accommodated the turntable also shown on the map. It was known as Belvedere Road. Charing Cross came near to closure in 1930 when a scheme to build a new terminus on the right of this picture was rejected by the Government. (J.Scrace)

←

8. The signal box had 107 levers in a power frame which replaced 130 mechanical levers on 27th June 1926. The box closed on 16th April 1976, when the London Bridge panel took control of the area - the DEMU from Hastings is seen arriving a few days later. These units were in use from 1957 until 1986. (J.Scrace)

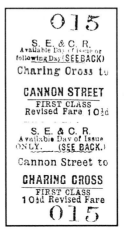

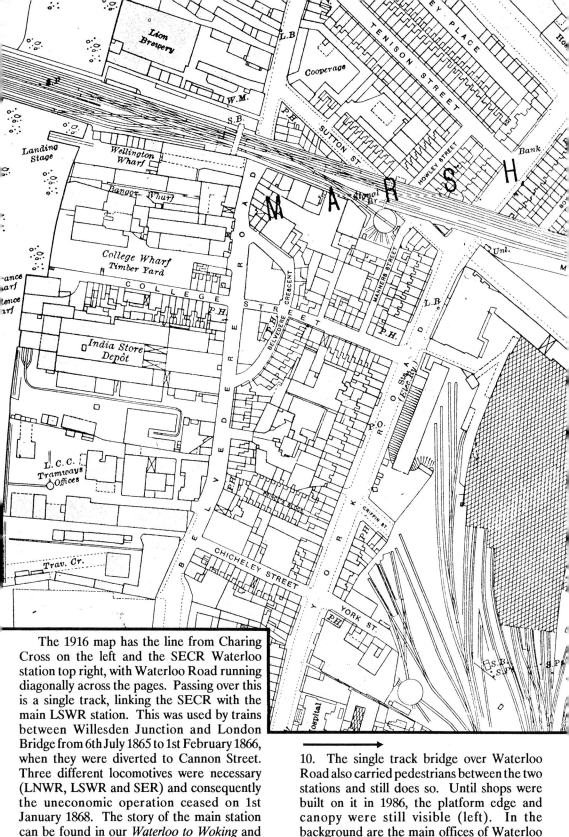

The 1916 map has the line from Charing Cross on the left and the SECR Waterloo station top right, with Waterloo Road running diagonally across the pages. Passing over this is a single track, linking the SECR with the main LSWR station. This was used by trains between Willesden Junction and London Bridge from 6th July 1865 to 1st February 1866, when they were diverted to Cannon Street. Three different locomotives were necessary (LNWR, LSWR and SER) and consequently the uneconomic operation ceased on 1st January 1868. The story of the main station can be found in our *Waterloo to Woking* and *Waterloo to Windsor* albums.

10. The single track bridge over Waterloo Road also carried pedestrians between the two stations and still does so. Until shops were built on it in 1986, the platform edge and canopy were still visible (left). In the background are the main offices of Waterloo station, built by the LSWR. (J.J.Smith)

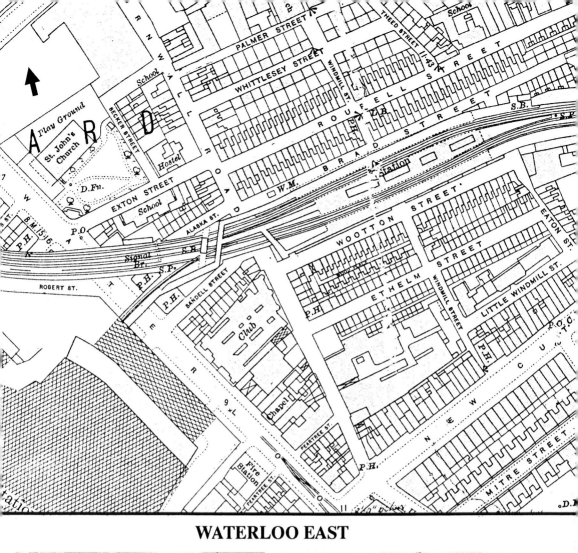

WATERLOO EAST

11. The station was opened on 1st January 1869 (five years after the line), although the little used connection to the LSWR was available from the outset. Named "Waterloo Junction" initially, it became "Eastern" on 7th July 1935 and "East" on 2nd May 1977. An eastbound train for the North Kent line via Greenwich is seen with class D1 no. 1502 on 24th February 1939. (H.C.Casserley)

12. The platforms are lettered to avoid confusion with the numbers of the main station, the majority of suburban trains using A and B. Ramsgate bound on 6th June 1961, one of the thirteen electric locomotives built for the Kent Coast electrification scheme, no. E5002, stands at platform C. (J.Scrace)

Initially only three tracks were provided (as marked) one being used by the Charing Cross - Cannon Street shuttle. A fourth one was opened on 2nd June 1901. The SER's Blackfriars station is marked as an island platform between Blackfriars Road and the LCDR's Metropolitan Extension line on this 1870 map, although it had closed on 1st January 1869. There was no connection here between the SER and the LCDR until 1st June 1878. A frequent service of trains between north and south-east London used it until 1917 but it was not until 1988 that this was restored under the name "Thameslink".

13. Metropolitan Junction derived its name from its link with the Metropolitan Extension of the LCDR. The box also controlled Cannon Street West Junction and was on the south side of the lines. Closure took place on 16th April 1976. The nearby Southwark Depot (for continental freight) and Ewer Street Depot (for locomotive coaling and turning) are illustrated in our *Charing Cross to Dartford* album, picture no. 16. (J.Scrace)

20

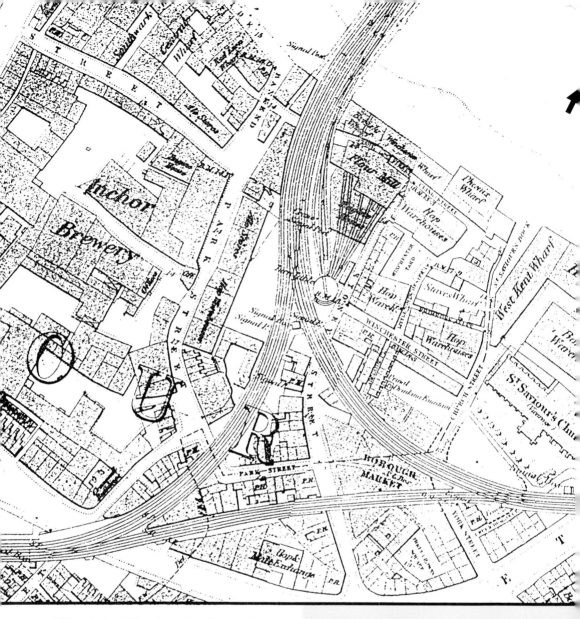

This 1870 edition has the five tracks to Cannon Street at the top, with three lines on each of the spurs - two up and one down. This, not surprisingly, caused severe operating difficulties. As most trains to Charing Cross ran via Cannon Street, there were serious delays and a number of collisions owing to the large number of conflicting movements and the great demand made on signalmen. Quadrupling of the right spur was completed in about 1916 but the double track over Borough Market continues to cause congestion in peak hours. The locomotive depot and turntable ceased to be used in 1926 and St. Saviour's Church (right) became Southwark Cathedral in 1905.

15. Initially the bridge carried five tracks and a footway with a halfpenny toll, this being open to the public between 1872 and 1877. From 1886 until 1893 work was in progress to widen the bridge on its west side to accommodate an additional five tracks. The first signal box had 67 levers but its successor, illustrated here, had 243 and was in use from 22nd April 1893 until 5th June 1926. No. 2 Box was at the south end of the bridge. By 1900, there were 398 arrivals on weekdays but most Charing Cross services ceased to call here after 31st December 1916. The east tower contained a water tank to provide hydraulic power and water for the locomotives. (National Railway Museum)

CANNON STREET

14. Above the entrance to the station, which opened on 1st September 1866, are the four floors of the City Terminus Hotel, which came into use in May 1867. Lacking continental passengers, it was not as successful as the Charing Cross Hotel and so the bedrooms were converted into railway offices in 1931 ("Southern House") but the public rooms were retained for banquets and meetings. (National Railway Museum)

16. Electric working of the Orpington, Bromley North, Addiscombe and Hayes services commenced on 28th February 1926, with only three platforms (left) electrified. No. 1 Box straddles eight tracks but there are ten parallel lines beyond it. No. 2 Box is in the distance, in line with the left-hand tracks. (British Rail)

17. Complete remodelling of the trackwork and platforms were necessary to accommodate further suburban electric services and so the station was closed from 5th until 28th June 1926 to allow this and the installation of colour light signalling to take place. (British Rail)

18. Platform renumbering took place, no. 1 henceforth being on the east side (right). Platforms 1 to 5 received conductor rails in 1926, nos. 6 and 7 in 1939 (for the Gillingham electrification) and no. 8 in 1959, when part of the Kent Coast was electrified. The original short platform (No. 4) was eliminated in the reconstruction. (British Rail)

19. Power operation meant that a smaller signal box could be built in 1926, its 143 miniature levers coming into use on 27th June. A fire in the ground floor relay room on 5th April 1957 partially destroyed the timber building and resulted in closure of the station completely for three days and partially for four weeks. (British Rail)

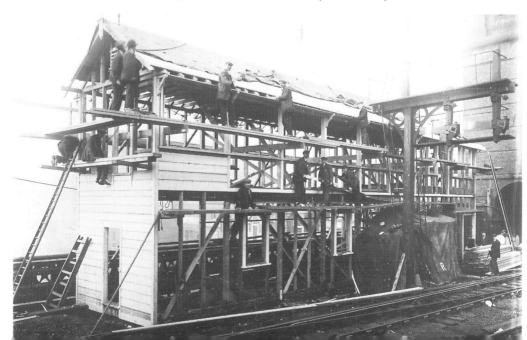

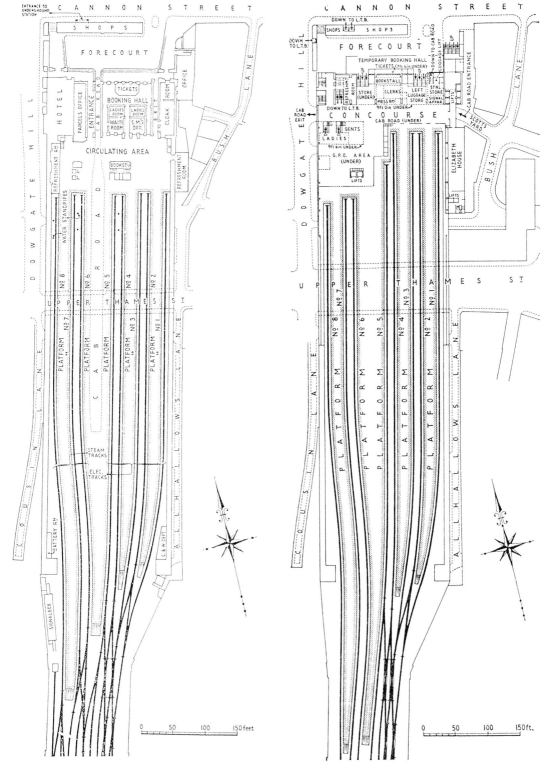

On the left is the arrangement following the 1926 alterations and on the right is the plan that resulted from the 1964 rebuilding. In connection with further major track alterations south of the station in readiness for 12-car Networker suburban trains, the station was closed from 22nd July to 22nd September 1991, except in peak hours. (Railway Magazine).

Extract from *War on the Line* relating to the German bombing in 1941.

20. On 9th April 1957, scaffolding surrounded the damaged part of the box (right), while temporary platform extension was taking place beyond the wagons. Ten-car suburban trains commenced running on 17th June 1957, permanent extension being completed in the following January. In the distance is brake van no. M730181 which was used as a temporary signal box. The old box was shortened, as seen in the next picture, and fitted with a 47-lever power frame adapted from a 225-lever unit in stock at Crewe. This short-term expedient was in use until a new box, at the south end of the bridge, was opened on 15th December 1957. (D.Cullum)

The night of May 10th-11th is another of *the* dates, and this time Cannon Street shall come first with its story of men huddled all night on the bridge, not merely with bombs falling all round them but with the lively expectation of themselves falling into the river. About 11 o'clock bombs and incendiaries began to drop in showers, and the foreman and a lineman went out into the thick of them to put out fires on the bridge. When they came back they found that two heavy H.E. bombs had fallen by the side of one of the tower on the platforms; the station hotel was on fire—it was ultimately gutted—and so was the station roof. As pieces from the blazing roof were falling everywhere it was decided that the safest plan for the trains standing in the station was on the bridge, and they were moved there accordingly. The safety was emphatically relative, for the bombs were streaming down into the growing fire; some fell in the river and the splash from one of them went over the signal-box. The men crouched on their engines or took the best available shelter in the tower on the bridge, making periodical dashes out of it to try to put out a fire in the van of one of the trains. After a while even the tower failed, owing to pieces of masonry falling inside it. There was nothing for it but the naked bridge from which the view became ever more tremendous with the wharves and warehouses by the station making one long line of fire beside the water's edge, while the fumes were so thick that it was hard to breathe.

Layout of Cannon Street Station platforms before the reorganisation of 1926. (Railway Magazine)

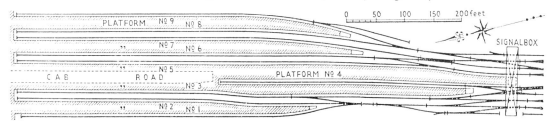

21. No. 30925 *Cheltenham* stands at platform 7 on 12th April 1958, with the 12.16 to Hastings, the platform having earlier been lengthened to accommodate 12-car trains. In late 1963, the 37ft long bridge over Upper Thames Street was replaced by 80ft long steel girders to allow for the construction of a dual carriageway. The massive roof lost its two acres of glass in WWII and the 1000 tons of Hawkshaw's ironwork was dismantled in 1958. (A.E.Bennett)

22. The trellis barriers were lost to allow platform lengthening for 10-car trains at the buffer end. The former cab road was latterly used for mail traffic but this was moved to a lower floor and lifts provided, thus allowing the demolition of the hotel/Southern House area in 1963. A new 15-storey office block replaced it and was opened in July 1965, the modern booking office being ready in December. (Lens of Sutton)

SOUTH OF CANNON STREET

24. A northward view on 17th June 1926 shows the lines from Metropolitan Junction in the foreground. On the left is Cannon Street No. 2 Box, which was built on piers and was partly over a turntable. The remains of another turntable are evident on the right, it becoming the site of the new signal box in 1957. Beyond it is the new sub-station, which replaced an engine shed. This location was known as Stoney Street Junction. (British Rail)

23. The towers are listed structures (Grade II) and received repairs and gilding in 1986. In June 1988, work started on the erection of nearly 9500 tonnes of steelwork to form a six storey building above the northern part of the platforms. The web of the main spine girder is an amazing 3.5m across. Much of the structure was prefabricated at Hither Green and transported by rail, the first of fifty 30 tonne columns arriving on 28th April 1989. Seen in August 1991, the upper part of the building has been angled to prevent obstruction of the view of St. Pauls Cathedral from London Bridge. (A.Dasi-Sutton)

25. The Cannon Street and Charing Cross lines converge at Borough Market Junction, in the shadow of Southwark Cathedral (right). An extremely busy box, it operated an unusual "paralleling" system at peak times, whereby two trains would run parallel to one another into Cannon Street while two were running out simultaneously, thus reducing junction occupation. The box closed on 16th April 1976 and is visible lower right. It handled around 100 trains per hour or 1000 a day! This compares with Clapham Junction's 2400 per day, but these ran largely parallel to one another and not over level junctions. Since 1976, most trains have crossed east of London Bridge resulting in the removal of the junction here during the summer of 1991. At this time, plans were being made for the quadrupling of the southern part of the triangle. (British Rail)

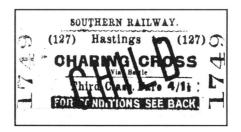

SOUTHERN RAILWAY.
(127) Hastings to (127)
CHARING CROSS
Via Battle
Third Class. Fare 4/1½
FOR CONDITIONS SEE BACK

26. On the other side of the triangle, an up Hastings train approaches Metropolitan Junction on 21st May 1937, having reversed at Cannon Street. No. 907 *Dulwich* is waiting for a London Bridge - Charing Cross service to clear the junction. In the 1950s, some empty stock working from Cannon Street was double headed on this spur prior to the steep climb to the former LCDR route, where a further reversal near the disused Ludgate Hill station would take place. (H.C.Casserley)

27. Having just passed the 35-lever Borough Market Junction box, London Bridge station comes into view from the rear of a Ferme Park (Eastern Region) to Hither Green transfer freight in 1956. The right hand part of the bridge over the station approach was added in about 1902. (V.Mitchell)

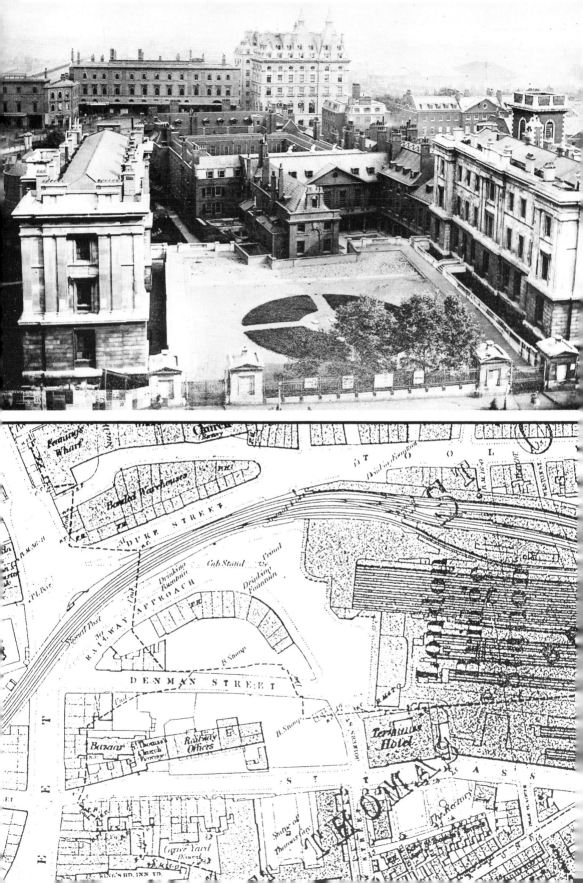

28. St Thomas' Hospital is seen from Borough Market Junction, with the background including London Bridge station (left), Terminus Hotel (centre) and Guy's Hospital (right). By the time the photograph was taken, the entire St. Thomas' Hospital was closed and belonged to the SER. The long legal battle which led to this is detailed by Adrian Gray in *South Eastern Railway* (Middleton Press 1990). The terrace with dormer windows (right) remained in use as railway offices until the 1960s. (Special Trustees for St. Thomas' Hospital)

LONDON BRIDGE

The 1870 map shows the lines from Borough Market Junction on the left. Denman Street had recently been constructed on the site of the north wing of St. Thomas' Hospital, the south wing being marked "Bazaar". The southernmost eleven platform lines were those of the London, Brighton & South Coast Railway, who had earlier inherited the termini of the London & Croydon and the London & Brighton. The former had exchanged stations with the London & Greenwich in 1840, some of the complexities of the resulting amalgam being shown in plans in our *London Bridge to East Croydon* and *Charing Cross to Dartford* albums.

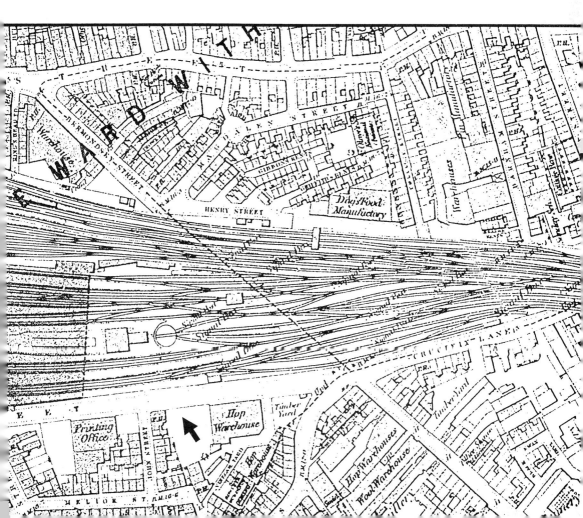

29. A down express enters platform 2 in July 1913, the third coach being a Pullman car. Viewed from platform 6, no. 5 road (lower right) was devoid of a platform and was used by up goods trains waiting for a path through Borough Market and Metropolitan Junctions on their way to northern lines. (H.J.Patterson Rutherford coll.)

30. Viewed from platform 2, E class no. 1515 runs east in the early 1930s with Birdcage stock, the headcode indicating the North Kent line via Greenwich. The scissors crossover was later replaced by a crossover from 3 to 2 only. The station offices on the left were severely damaged by bombing during WWII. (D.Cullum coll.)

31. No. 30903 *Charterhouse* climbs the 1 in 103 gradient into platform 7 with the straight-sided Hastings line stock on 29th April 1954, while old and new suburban electrics run into platform 4. On the right are the four ex-SECR terminal platforms, the former LBSCR lines being to the right of the signal box and water tank. (R.C.Riley)

32. The northern part was extensively remodelled prior to WWI, the overall roof over the terminal platforms being removed and their numbers reduced. From 1864 until 1901, this area had been used as the Continental Goods Depot. Three island platforms were provided for through services and two foot-bridges connected them with the low level platforms. This view from the eastern one in April 1953 was taken soon after the removal of the through goods line and shows the realignment of platform 4. A new canopy followed. (D.Cullum)

33. A Tunbridge Wells West service via Oxted stands at platform 10 on 1st April 1954, while the usual mail vans wait at the short platform 11. Note that platform 9 was the only one to be provided with an engine release crossover. (H.C.Casserley)

34. Opposite platform 7 was a short, low, unnumbered platform known as "The Mount" and used exclusively for mail traffic. The sharp curve and steep gradient often presented locomotives with a starting problem. A following electric sometimes had to provide assistance at the rear. (E.Wilmshurst)

36. The through platforms were realigned and renumbered, and a single footbridge was provided. Sadly, this has all the disadvantages of underground travel - inadequate ventilation and no view. The 10.03 Charing Cross to Ashford stands at platform 5 on 29th June 1977, its next stop being Orpington. This platform was signalled for reversible running, as were nos. 2 and 4. (J.Scrace)

35. This and the previous photograph were taken in 1971, this one emphasising the need for rebuilding following the devastation of WWII. Reconstruction took place in 1975-78, platforms 20-22 closing on 31st July 1972 in readiness for the track alterations and the construction of a new signal box on their site. (E.Wilmshurst)

37. 2EBP no. 6261 heads empty stock on 5th July 1991 on the through up line, which was brought into use on 19th April 1976. Platform 7 is closed and work is in progress to widen the formation to allow for the provision of an additional high level track. Two tracks and a new island platform are planned in connection with the quadrupling over Borough Market. This would allow Thameslink services to use this route throughout the day. (V.Mitchell)

Diagram of the track layout in 1976.

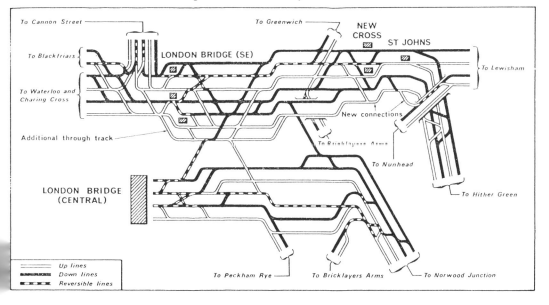

SPA ROAD

38. This was the first and temporary terminus of the London & Greenwich Railway, serving that purpose from 8th February until 14th December 1836. It reopened in October 1842 and was in use until February 1843 when a permanent structure was opened. This was replaced by a new station in 1867.

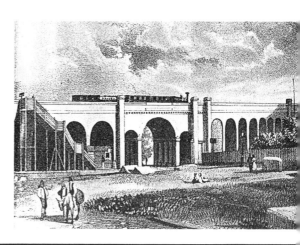

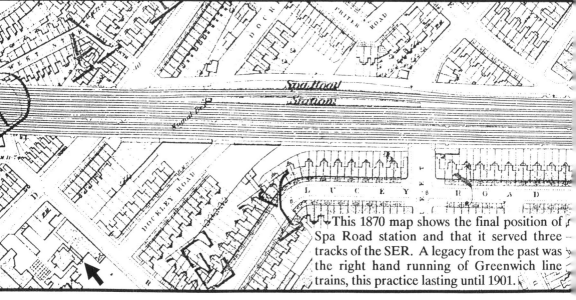

This 1870 map shows the final position of Spa Road station and that it served three tracks of the SER. A legacy from the past was the right hand running of Greenwich line trains, this practice lasting until 1901.

39. A photograph from 6th September 1940 shows some bomb damage at the site of Spa Road station, which had despatched its last passenger during the previous war, on 15th March 1915. A similar station at Southwark Park, near Corbetts Lane Junction, was in use until the same date, having opened on 1st October 1902. (British Rail)

40. The 3.30pm empty stock from Rotherhithe Road Carriage Depot to Charing Cross on 25th September 1956 is passing under the former LBSCR main line to East Croydon. The depot is marked on the next map, top left of the right page. (J.J.Smith)

41. Turning round a few minutes later, we see the train from the previous picture approaching Surrey Canal Junction with no.34084 *253 Squadron* at the rear. Behind it is more empty stock, hauled by no.31287, a C class 0-6-0. Both trains would reverse at North Kent East Junction to reach the London termini. (J.J.Smith)

The 6" to 1 mile map of 1916 has the lines from London Bridge at the top of this page, with Bricklayers Arms goods lines below them. Opposite (top right) is the Deptford Wharf branch, while the Surrey Docks station on the East London Line is at the top. On the right is the line to Greenwich and below it the SECR New Cross station on the line to Lewisham. Lower centre is the LBSCR New Cross station (now New Cross Gate) on the line to East Croydon.

42. North Kent East Box was in use from 1929 until 1976, its predecessor being shown in picture 41 in *Charing Cross to Dartford*. It was situated just to the south of the Surrey Canal, which runs across the middle of the page opposite and which is described in *Surrey Waterways* (Middleton Press 1987). The Greenwich and New Cross lines part company here. (J.Scrace)

NEW CROSS

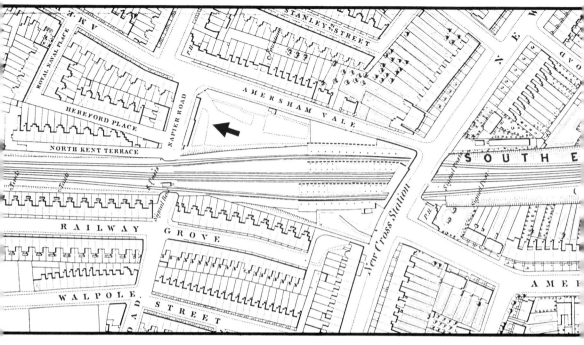

The 1869 survey reveals that there were six platform faces for the four tracks. A single line for East London trains was laid in 1876, parallel to North Kent Terrace.

43. The complexity of the signalling at the London end of the station was due to the junction with the East London Line. There were connections on both the up and down sides. (Lens of Sutton)

44. The up East London connection is on the left as no. 30923 *Bradfield* speeds through with a Dover train on 15th September 1957. On the extreme right is the London Transport single line for East London trains. (A.E.Bennett)

45. A 1967 photograph shows the main entrance on the road bridge. New timber buildings were erected on the down side in 1975 and this symmetrical structure was demolished. The station was "New Cross & Naval School" until 1854, when it became "New Cross (SER)", the suffix distinguishing it from "New Cross (LBSCR)". The latter became "New Cross Gate" in 1923 and the suffixes were dropped. (J.N.Faulkner)

46. A down freight, hauled by no. 73006, passes under the temporary footbridge on 4th September 1975, while reconstruction was in progress. This resulted in only three through platforms; the building on the left is being demolished. (J.Scrace)

47. During reconstruction a subway was built, the platforms were redesignated A to D and the roadbridge was widened and lengthened to pass over five tracks. In 1985, the canopy was extended towards the camera and a brick and glass building replaced the timber one at a cost of £1/2m. The LT train will pass under the main line twice before heading north. (C.R.L.Coles)

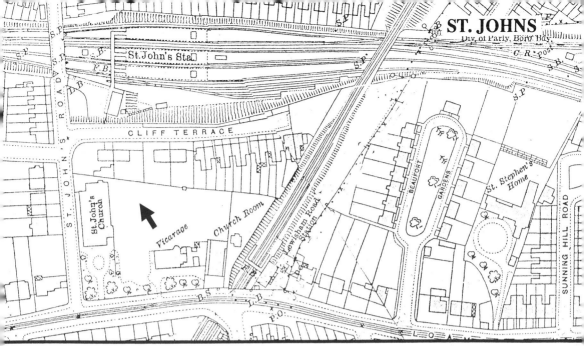

The station opened on 1st June 1873. On the left of this 1916 edition are the four tracks from New Cross, which pass through the 87yd long Tanners Hill Tunnel. The station has six platform faces, the lower one being a bay which was abolished in 1926. On the right is the double track to Lewisham and the four direct lines to Hither Green, two of which came into use on 1st July 1865. From top to bottom is the Greenwich Park branch, which is featured in our *Holborn Viaduct to Lewisham* album. Picture 116 therein was taken from the same location as the one below, but 45 years later.

48. This 1913 view shows Lewisham trains on the left and an up express on the right. Also evident are the buffers of the bay line. The northern abutment of the former LCDR overbridge is still visible today. (H.J.Patterson Rutherford coll.)

49. No. 921 *Shrewsbury* is on the down fast line while 3SUB no. 1766 stops with a Sevenoaks service. The third island platform, shown on the map, has been removed. (H.N.James)

50. A fence and cables run along the remains of the third platform, as no. 938 *St. Olave's* speeds towards London showing the Hastings headcode. In the background is the 1929 signal box and opposite it is the bridge for the Lewisham - Nunhead line, opened in the same year to carry north-south freight transfer traffic. These slow trains could travel via Loughborough Junction and reduce congestion in the London Bridge area. (H.N.James)

51. The bridge collapsed on 4th December 1957 when the 4.56pm Cannon Street to Ramsgate ran into the rear of the 5.18pm Charing Cross to Hayes under the structure. This is the scene three days after the disaster - the buckled span had to be completely renewed, its replacement still being in use today. (A.E.Bennett)

52. The little used island platform on the fast lines was removed in September 1973 and the curve in the up line eliminated. On the right, an up train emerges from under the bridge that was the scene of the Lewisham disaster. A bidirectional spur on a 1 in 45 gradient was laid just beyond the right margin of this picture and opened on 29th March 1976 as part of the improvements of the mid-1970s. A new station building was opened in August 1983. (J.Scrace)

LEWISHAM

53. Looking from the end of the centre platform towards St. Johns in 1928, the bridge seen in picture 48 is in the distance. Lewisham Junction box was braced and moved back 25ft. to give space for the new lines to Nunhead. Telegraph history was made here on 2nd November 1852, when the Greenwich Observatory started transmitting its time signal through the SER's wires. The nation's clocks were synchronised for the first time and Bristol had to advance its timepieces by 14 minutes, amidst howls of protest. (I.Gotheridge coll.)

54. In the summer of 1987, diesel railcars were run regularly as part of a driver route learning programme associated with the commencement of Thameslink services in the following May. No. L101 is running between St. Johns and Hither Green. The Nunhead lines are on the left, these coming into use for freight traffic on 7th July 1929. The massive sub-station is in the background. (J.Scrace)

55. The Blackheath line is on the left and the Nunhead route is on the right as we look towards the sharply curved platforms for Hither Green trains. Although intended as a freight route, the Nunhead line was used by electric trains to Holborn Viaduct from 30th September 1935. (V.Mitchell)

56. A second photograph from June 1991 shows the renovated exterior which is at the top of an inclined approach road. The first station on the site opened on 30th July 1849, being served by trains on the Woolwich route. It was replaced in 1856 by a junction station in readiness for trains on the Mid-Kent line to Beckenham. The name "Lewisham Junction" was then used until 1929. (V.Mitchell)

SOUTH OF LEWISHAM

Diagram of the lines and junctions in the Lewisham area.

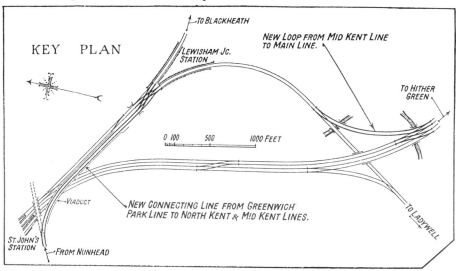

KEY PLAN

TO BLACKHEATH

LEWISHAM JC. STATION

NEW LOOP FROM MID KENT LINE TO MAIN LINE.

TO HITHER GREEN

0 100   500   1000 FEET

TO LADYWELL

VIADUCT

NEW CONNECTING LINE FROM GREENWICH PARK LINE TO NORTH KENT & MID KENT LINES.

ST. JOHN'S STATION   FROM NUNHEAD

←

57. The station approach is between the empty aggregate wagons and the tapered white building. The locomotives on 9th July 1987 were nos. 33207 and 33060. An up local train stands at platform 1, the massive brick base of its waiting shelter being evident. (J.Scrace)

58. Parks Bridge Junction is seen from the north in 1944, with the Ladywell Loop to Ladywell on the right. This came into use in September 1866 and allowed trains from London to reach the 1857 route to Beckenham without passing through Lewisham.
(British Rail)

59. A southbound train has just passed over Lewisham High Street and runs parallel to Courthill Road as work is in progress on quadrupling the tracks. This was completed between New Cross and Hither Green in 1904.
(Lens of Sutton)

HITHER GREEN

The Dartford Loop line through Sidcup (top right) opened on 1st September 1866 but a station at the junction was not opened until 1st June 1895. The avenue terminating at the embankment is now part of Nightingale Grove. This is the first edition from about 1870.

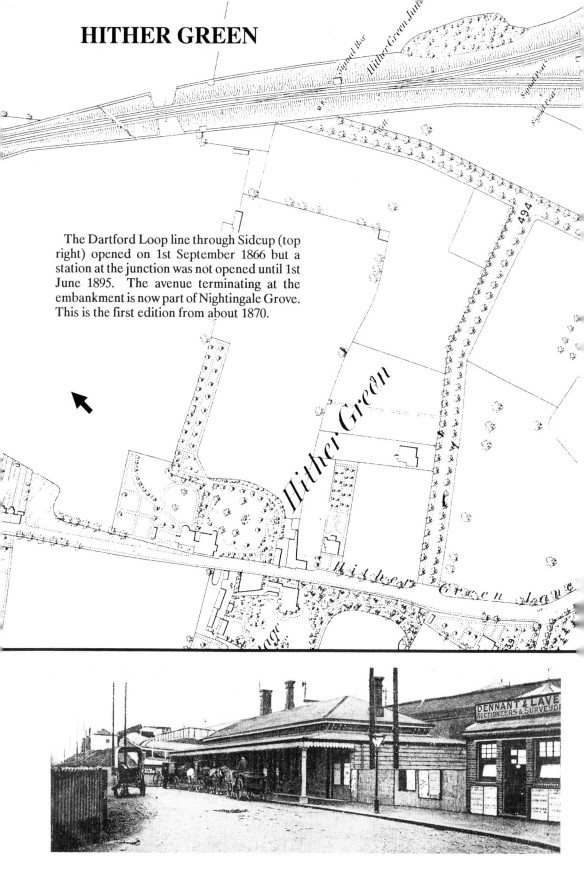

A map and other photographs of this station can be found in the companion album *Lewisham to Dartford*, which includes the Sidcup and Bexleyheath lines.

61. Seen in 1938, class L1 no. 1787 is about to pass over the subway linking the platforms. The subway is still in use but the covered access (right) to the island platform is closed. Note the once popular concrete signal post. (H.N.James)

60. The SER provided entrances at the north end of the station (as now) but the developer of the St. Germains area was dissatisfied with this and paid for the building and entrance seen here. It was in Springbank Road, at the south end of the present up fast platform. (Lens of Sutton)

62. The Springbank Road entrance is on the left, Hither Green Station "A" Box in the distance and "B" Box on the right. Both boxes closed on 4th February 1962, six months after this photograph had been taken. (British Rail)

63. A 1961 southward view from the footbridge seen in the previous picture includes the then new diesel oil tanks of the locomotive depot. "The Man of Kent" is hauled by nos. D6500 and D5010, the latter providing steam heating for the coaches. No. D5013 waits to leave the marshalling yard, the track to the left of it being the reception road. (J.N.Faulkner)

64. In 1974 a new booking hall was built between platforms 4 and 5, and platforms 1 to 4 received new canopies and a footbridge. On the right is the old footbridge linking platforms 5 and 6 on the Sidcup line to Dartford. The train passing is the 13.05 Charing Cross to Ashford on 16th March 1985. (D.Brown)

HITHER GREEN DEPOT

65. Opened on 10th September 1933, the six-road shed was built largely of concrete and founded on 470 concrete piles. Additional sorting sidings and a 65ft turntable were also provided at this time. C class no. 1711 was recorded on 4th March 1939. (H.C.Casserley)

66. The photographer turned and pictured another C class. It is running south on the Lee Spur towards Hither Green Sidings "A" Box. This connection between the Sidcup and Orpington lines came into full use on 30th April 1905 and provided a means of minimising the number of freight trains in the London area. (H.C.Casserley)

67. A 1956 view of the yard includes the prominent water treatment tower and the water tank, partly obscured by escaping steam. Water was raised from a 350ft deep well sunk into the underlying chalk. Water used for boiler washout was subsequently filtered, cleaned and reused. On the right is the elevated siding serving the coal stage and in the centre are two of the class W 2-6-4Ts used on transfer freight work. (A.E.Bennett)

68. From its inception, the depot has almost exclusively supplied locomotives for freight work. Here is an exception. No. 73001 is standing in the refuelling shed on 21st August 1985, its duty being to work the Venice-Simplon-Orient Express between Victoria and Folkestone Harbour. (G.Lovell)

69. The old and the new are seen on 27th April 1990. Pairs of class 33s, such as 33008 and 33201 on the right, were for long used on the heavy mineral trains passing through the district. The powerful class 60 had just been introduced and one is able to do the work of two 33s. No. 60006 is evident; as is the original iron water tank. (J.Scrace)

70. From left to right in this March 1991 view is the yard departure road, the arrival road, the signal box (opened 4th Feburary 1962, closed 6th November 1976), the locomotive depot, the civil engineering yard and the Lee Spur from the Dartford Loop. (M.Turvey)

SOUTH OF HITHER GREEN

71. A southward view in October 1945 includes Hither Green Sidings "C" Box, the four electrified main lines and part of the massive Hither Green Marshalling Yard. This had been started in 1899 and was progressively expanded, until in 1929 it was receiving about 40 trains per day from the LMS and LNER via Farringdon and 20 to 30 from the LMS and GWR via the West London Line, plus a large number from Feltham Yard. The yard reached its optimum in 1933, when there were 11 parallel lines on the up side, plus 29 on the down side. (British Rail)

72. The extensive Hither Green Continental Depot was constructed at the north end of the up sidings and opened in October 1960. The poles to the left of it carried wires which supplied current to electric locomotives built for the Kent Coast electrification. One of the thirteen is seen in picture 12, with its pantograph retracted. The wires ended at the gantry near the corner of the building. The depot closed in February 1987 and was demolished the following year. The yard in the foreground closed in January 1985. (British Rail)

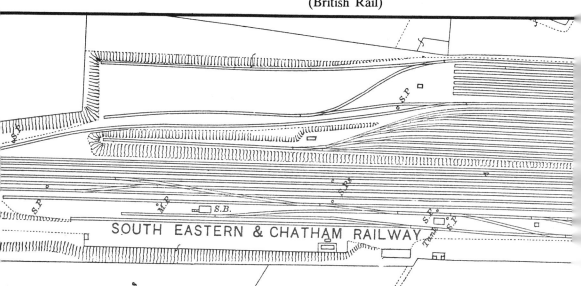

SOUTH EASTERN & CHATHAM RAILWAY

On the left of this 1916 map are the six lines seen in picture no. 63 and above the word EASTERN is Hither Green Sidings "B" Box. "C" Box was just beyond the right border, both closing on 4th February 1962.

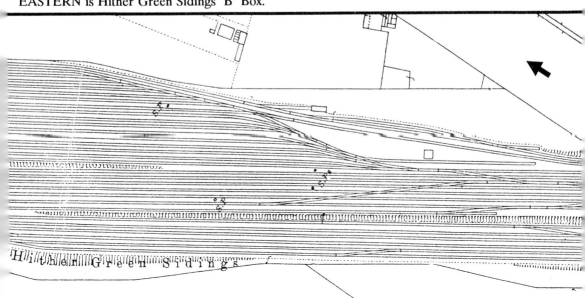

Hither Green Sidings

73. During 1991 the sites of the sidings on both sides of the main line were relevelled by laser, and eight new sidings laid each side for the new 12-car Networker trains. The two sides will be linked by a footbridge removed from New Cross Gate. On the left is the washing machine on the line to Grove Park Depot, seen in the next photograph. (M.Turvey)

74. On the down side, north of Grove Park station, a shed and berthing sidings were provided for EMUs as part of the Kent Coast electrification scheme. The depot was energised on 25th May 1959. (M.Turvey)

75. Hither Green Sidings "C" Box is in the distance, as a down express passes the entrance to the sidings of Holland, Hannen & Cubitts, builders of the LCC's Grove Park Housing Estate. Their line was in use from 23rd June 1924 until 2nd May 1937. (Revd.A.W.V.Mace)

76. On the right is the gate seen in the previous picture. In the centre is the locomotive shed and outside it stands the contractors' saddle tank. The line to the building site curves past the coaling stage. (J.W.Sparrowe)

GROVE PARK

The station was opened on 1st November 1871, over £1500 having been provided towards the cost by Mr. Pond, a local landowner. This 1916 map shows the complex junction with the Bromley North branch, which runs off the lower right corner.

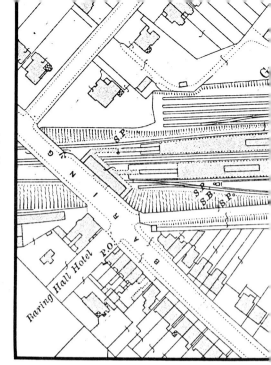

77. A down goods train approaches the branch signals, some time before the quadrupling in the early years of this century. On the right are the sidings which were mainly used for berthing empty coaches between the peak periods. They were still in place in the 1970s but were never electrified.
(I.Gotheridge coll.)

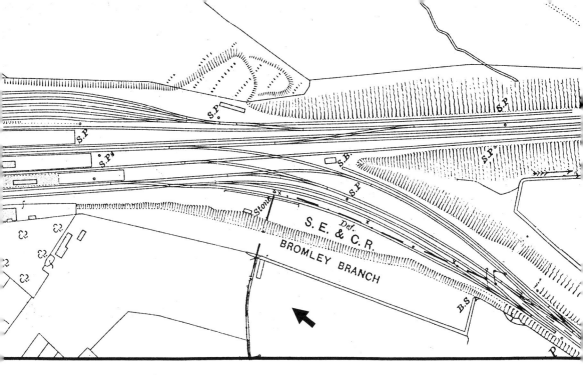

78. Improvements in 1892 included a new waiting room and a roof to the footbridge. Note that the leading brake van contains both roof and side lookouts - birdcage and ducket. D class no. 726 entered traffic in February 1901. (D.Cullum coll.)

79. Another pre-quadrupling picture shows class D no. 733, also completed in 1901, passing the junction box. Its successor was built in 1905 and destroyed by fire on 23rd August 1938, when it contained 31 full size levers and 44 slides for working signals electrically. Within 12 days the box was extended, repaired and fitted with a new 60-lever locking frame. (Lens of Sutton)

80. The station was rebuilt in 1905 and remains little altered today, except that the platform on the right now has a fence adjacent to the train and a footbridge leading up to the camera position. This structure was erected in about 1962. (Lens of Sutton)

81. The down through starting signals were unusually low so that they were not obscured by the platform canopy and the road bridge. The dilapidated coach bodies were provided for staff accommodation. On the right, a down local electric runs into one of the two parallel Chislehurst Tunnels. (J.H.Aston)

82. The Bromley North branch shuttle train waits at platform 1 on 28th August 1990, a two car EPB being sufficient for off-peak services. The connection to the branch at the far end of the platforms ceased to be used in November 1988. A single goods siding was earlier situated to the right of the train, this being taken out of use on 4th December 1961. (J.Scrace)

Bromley North Branch   SUNDRIDGE PARK

83. A down train enters the station, which was opened with the branch on 1st January 1878 and named "Plaistow" until 1st July 1894. Mr Scott was the local landowner concerned with the provision of this station. (Lens of Sutton)

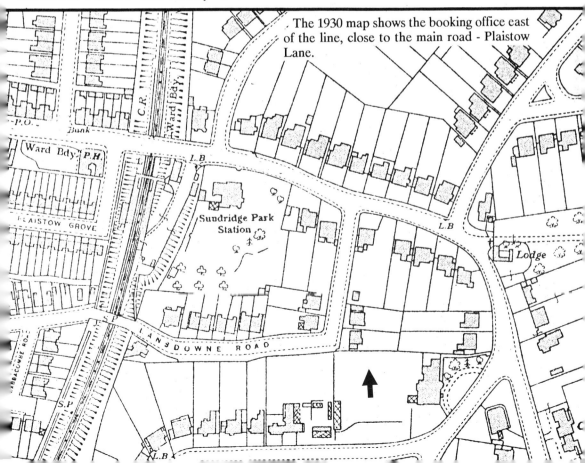

. The 1930 map shows the booking office east of the line, close to the main road - Plaistow Lane.

84. Photographed in 1987, the booking office was a rare example of a surviving SER all-timber building. Almost level access was provided from the main road (right) to the footbridge span on the left. The granite setts were provided as a durable surface on which horses and their narrow wheeled vehicles could stand. As the animals were not house trained, an easy-clean surface was useful. (G.Lovell)

85. An August 1990 view shows that only the down side canopy had been lost. On the right is the booking office, situated at the top of the roadway once used for turning horse-drawn carriages. Both booking offices on the branch were still staffed, although the distance between the two stations is under 800 yds. The station has been closed on Sundays since 1962. (J.Scrace)

BROMLEY NORTH

86. When opened on 1st January 1878, the station was named "Bromley SER". Following the formation of the SECR, it received its present name on 1st June 1899. Although the branch was double track from the outset, the station had many features of a typical country branch line terminus. The foot crossing linked the two platforms, the up one having the larger canopy. (Lens of Sutton)

87. The SER was noted for its lack of consideration for passengers and inadequate stations. It appears that the old coach body was provided as an extension to the goods office and that it had a defective roof. At least passengers had a clean footway alongside the filthy road. The goods crane was of 7-ton capacity and was one of the few in the district. (R.C.Riley coll.)

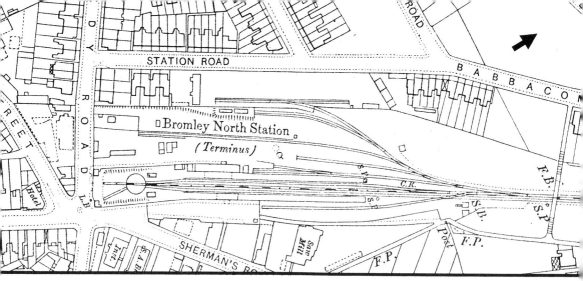

The 1912 survey includes a gated private siding, which terminated in the local council yard until 1926. The footbridge on the right replaced a level crossing in about 1900.

88. The SR eliminated all traces of the first station. The scene on 30th August 1925 included a temporary platform in the foreground. The first trial trip of an electric train took place on 19th November of that year. (British Rail)

89. An official photograph shows the early style of SR architecture, as seen at Margate and Ramsgate before they chose to use flat roofs and rounded corners. The Austin 7 may have been basic road transport but the station was far from basic with its copper-clad dome. (British Rail)

The 1933 edition shows the effect of the 1925 rebuilding and siding extensions. Note the large number of coal staithes required for the increasing number of hearths.

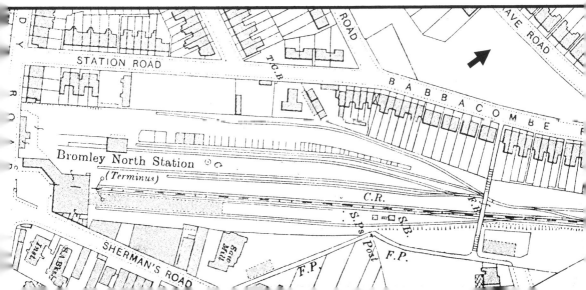

90. Standing at platform 1 are two 3SUBs with two trailer coaches between them, the furthest unit standing on the crossover used to release locomotives of parcels and goods trains. In the electrified siding there is a 3SUB and two coaches, the other unit working an off-peak service. The release line eventually became the berthing siding, the others being lifted to make way for a car park. Goods traffic ceased on 20th May 1968. (Lens of Sutton)

91. Seen in the 1960s, the terminus retained many SR features, including the hexagonal lightshades. Trellis barriers, once common at the SR London termini, were still retained at Bromley North in 1991. (Lens of Sutton)

92. Platform extension in 1954 surrounded the old signalbox and in 1959 a new flat-roofed one was built close to the footbridge, this being the signalman's view. The signal gantry over the 10-coach train on 30th August 1990 also once spanned a berthing siding. The box did not have to be staffed outside peak hours, as the points at the end of platform 2 were automatic. (J.Scrace)

February 1890

	Week Days		Sundays

Down.
Charing Crs
Waterloo J.
Cannon St.
London Bdg
New Cross
St. John's
Grove Park
Plaistow
Bromley arr

Up.
Bromley dp
Plaistow
Grove Pk
St. John's
New Cross
London Bdg
Cannon St.
Waterloo J
Charng Cross

ELMSTEAD WOODS

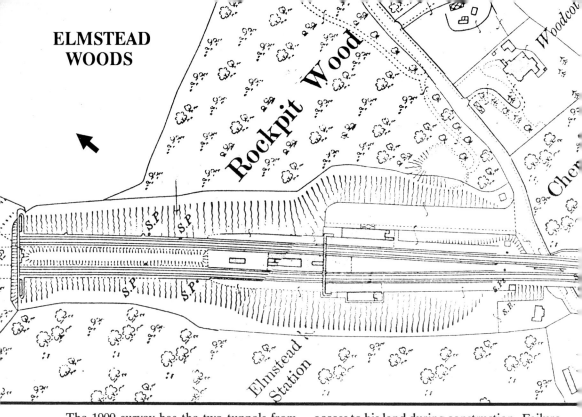

The 1909 survey has the two tunnels from Grove Park on the left. The northern one is 649 yds in length, the southern one being 591 yds. Neither were necessary from an engineering point of view, as there is only 4ft covering of earth in some places. They were demanded by the landowner who even refused access to his land during construction. Failure of the original (northern) one occurred on 17th July 1903, while the other was being built, and services were interrupted until 3rd November of that year, some trains being diverted via Oxted and Penshurst.

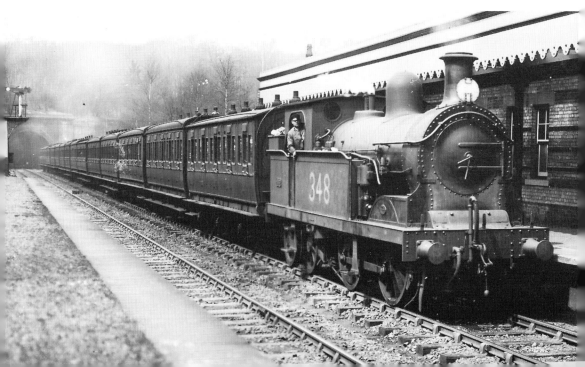

94. Generous provision was made for passengers, many of whom travelled first class. The "Schools" class were the most powerful 4-4-0s and were popular locomotives. No. 919 *Harrow* is bound for Dover, its train including one Pullman Car, painted chocolate and cream unlike those seen earlier in this album. (Lens of Sutton)

93. Opened as "Elmstead" on 1st July 1904, "Woods" was added on 1st October 1908. Emerging from the younger tunnel is a train of thirteen 6-wheelers, hauled by class Q1 0-4-4T no. 348, rebuilt from a domeless Q class in 1914. (Lens of Sutton)

95. A 1991 picture from the same location as the previous one includes a train bound for Ashford. The footbridge roof has been cut back and, not revealed, the up through platform buildings have been removed. (M.Turvey)

CHISLEHURST

96. The main buildings are on the down side and remain little altered today, apart from the loss of the ornamental ironwork. The massive telegraph poles have gone - the SER sold their telegraph system to the GPO in 1870 for £200,000. (Lens of Sutton)

The 1897 edition shows the small goods yard which was adjacent to the original station. This was a terminus from 1865 until 1868. Its relationship to the present station is shown on the next map.

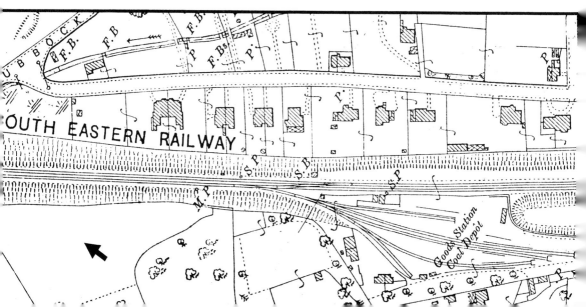

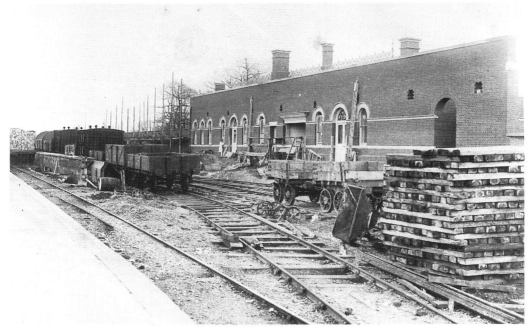

97. This is the state of progress on 1st March 1901, on the up side during the quadrupling work. Being on the through platform, the buildings were little used and no longer exist.

The suffix "and Bickley Park" was applied from the opening of the original station on 1st July 1865 until 1st September 1866. (British Rail)

98. A view from Summer Hill Road, at the south end of the station, on the same day shows the same building. The roadway served the

end loading dock shown on the map and is now heavily wooded. (British Rail)

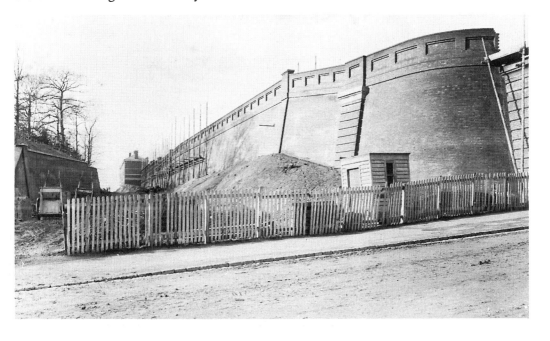

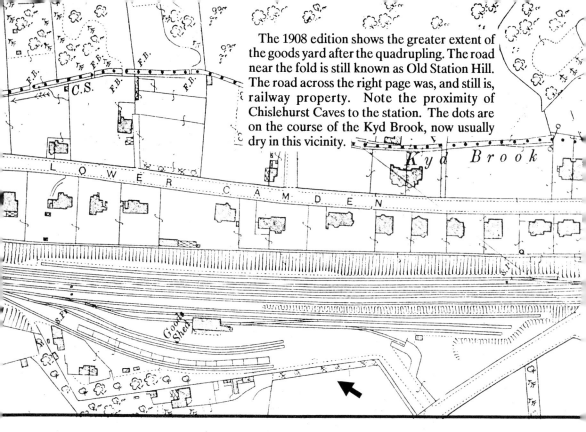

The 1908 edition shows the greater extent of the goods yard after the quadrupling. The road near the fold is still known as Old Station Hill. The road across the right page was, and still is, railway property. Note the proximity of Chislehurst Caves to the station. The dots are on the course of the Kyd Brook, now usually dry in this vicinity.

99. At the far end of the island platform in this 1914 picture is Chislehurst Junction Box. It controlled the then little used connections between the local and through lines, partly shown on the right of the map. At about this time the nearby Chislehurst Caves were used for storage of ammunition produced at Woolwich Arsenal. (D.Cullum coll.)

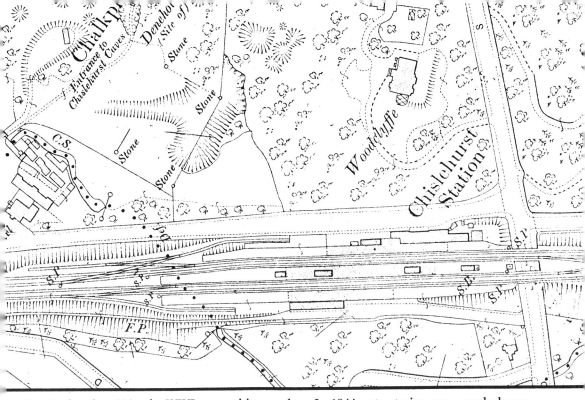

100. During the 1930s, the WWI ammunition railway in Chislehurst Caves was used in connection with mushroom growing but the battery electric locomotives were replaced by an Austin 7. During parts of WWII, the caves were used as air raid shelters by up to 15,000 people each night, most travelling by train each day. In 1944, extra trains were regularly run from Cannon Street in the evening. The 22 miles of passages made by man over many centuries, now attract a great number of visitors, some arriving by rail.
(Chislehurst Caves coll.)

101. On 16th May 1959, the down "Man of Kent" passes Chislehurst Goods box hauled by a grimy "West Country", no. 34005 *Barnstaple*. This train once carried an imposing headboard but lack of labour and enthusiasm was a problem by then. (S.C.Nash)

102. In addition to working the nearby crossovers, the box controlled the divergence of the Orpington and Chatham routes. Along with the Goods Box, it closed on 31st May 1959, when colour light signals were introduced. (Lens of Sutton)

SOUTHERN RAILWAY.
Available on DAY of issue ONLY.
PRIVILEGE MARKETING TICKET.
TRAFFIC DEPARTMENT
Orpington to
**BROMLEY SOUTH
AND BACK.**
Third Class
FOR CONDITIONS SEE BACK

5201

103. The two staff cottages were built in 1878 and to the left of them is a water tank which supplied the column visible through the signal gantry. Goods facilities were withdrawn on 18th November 1986 but two sidings were still in use in 1991 for ARC mineral traffic, ballast coming from Lydd for many years. (British Rail)

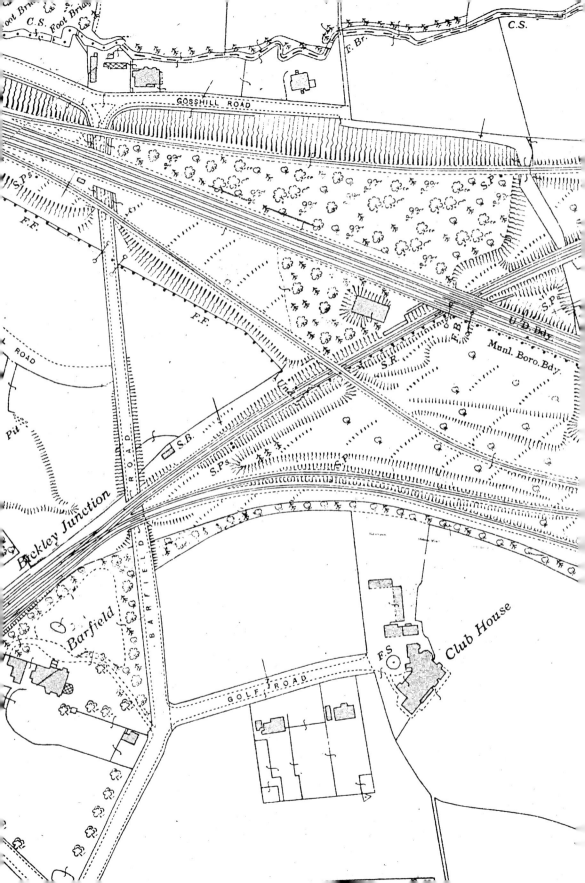

C.S. Foot Bridge

C.S.

F. Br.

C.S.

GOSSHILL ROAD

S. P.

S. P.

S.Ps.

F. B.

S. P.

U. D. Bdy.

F. E.

S. R.

Munl. Boro. Bdy.

ROAD

F. E.

Pit

S. B.

S.Ps.

Bickley Junction

Club House

F.S.

Barfield

BARFIELD ROAD

GOLF ROAD

S. R.
DOWN CHISLEHURST LOOP

M.P

Def

F.F. SO

Top left on this 1937 map are the lines from
Chislehurst Junction. The quadruple track
runs to the lower right and on to Petts Wood
Junction and Orpington. Lower left is Bickley
Junction, the former LCDR route running to
the top right and on to Chatham. The addition
of two loops in 1902 was one of the early and
important benefits of the 1899 merger of the
rival SER and LCDR. Precise dates are given
on the diagram overleaf.

M o o r
G r o v e

S. R.
UP CHISLEHURST LOOP

M.P

M.P

S.P.W.

M.P

S. R.
DOWN BICKLEY LOOP

S.P.W.

S.P. M.P

S. R.
UP BICKLEY LOOP

B.P.

S.P.

M.P

S.P.

Blackbrook Wood

104. The 3SUB is on the local line to Chislehurst while class L1 no. A756 overtakes it on the main line, as they pass Orpington Junction Box on 28th March 1929. The box was renamed "Petts Wood Junction" on 8th June 1936. (H.C.Casserley)

105. Two 3SUBs with trailers have just run onto the up Bickley Loop, working an Orpington to Victoria service on 18th April 1931. No time was lost in starting work on building the spurs, good progress being reported within 12 months of the formation of the SECR. (H.C.Casserley)

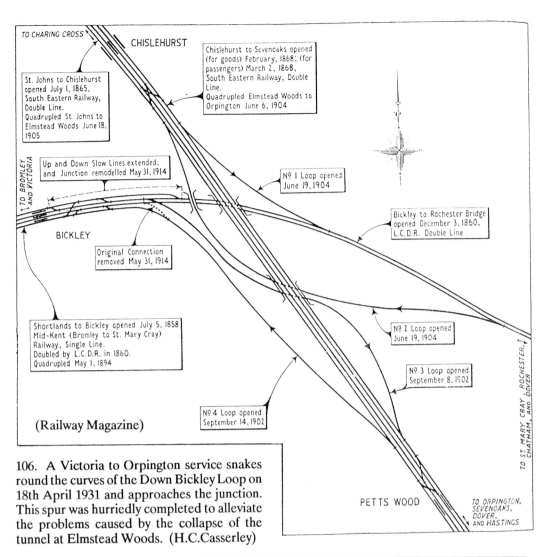

TO CHARING CROSS

CHISLEHURST

St. Johns to Chislehurst
opened July 1, 1865,
South Eastern Railway,
Double Line.
Quadrupled St. Johns to
Elmstead Woods June 18,
1905

Chislehurst to Sevenoaks opened
(for goods) February, 1868; (for
passengers) March 2, 1868,
South Eastern Railway, Double
Line.
Quadrupled Elmstead Woods to
Orpington June 6, 1904

TO BROMLEY AND VICTORIA

Up and Down Slow Lines extended,
and Junction remodelled May 31, 1914

Nº 1 Loop opened
June 19, 1904

Bickley to Rochester Bridge
opened December 3, 1860.
L.C.D.R. Double Line.

BICKLEY

Original Connection
removed May 31, 1914

Shortlands to Bickley opened July 5, 1858
Mid-Kent (Bromley to St. Mary Cray)
Railway, Single Line.
Doubled by L.C.D.R. in 1860.
Quadrupled May 1, 1894

Nº 2 Loop opened
June 19, 1904

Nº 3 Loop opened
September 8, 1902

(Railway Magazine)

Nº 4 Loop opened
September 14, 1902

TO ST. MARY CRAY, ROCHESTER, CHATHAM, AND DOVER

PETTS WOOD

TO ORPINGTON,
SEVENOAKS,
DOVER,
AND HASTINGS

106. A Victoria to Orpington service snakes
round the curves of the Down Bickley Loop on
18th April 1931 and approaches the junction.
This spur was hurriedly completed to alleviate
the problems caused by the collapse of the
tunnel at Elmstead Woods. (H.C.Casserley)

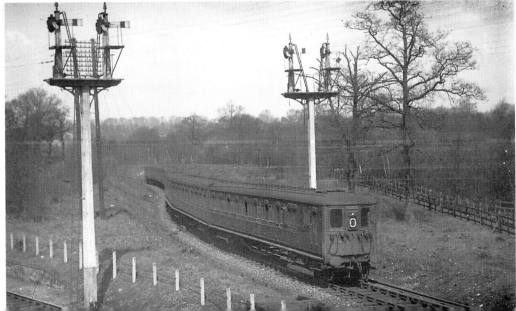

107. Class W 2-6-4T no. 31913 is on the down main line on 28th March 1953, hauling empty wagons to Knockholt. A temporary quarry had been opened there to provide chalk for constructing a wall to protect the Faversham - Margate main line, which had been destroyed by catastrophic floods. Details are shown in our *Sittingbourne to Ramsgate* album. (D.Cullum)

108. Looking south on the same day, from the signal seen in the centre of the previous photograph, we see the Petts Wood Junction Box, the station being in the distance. The box replaced the one seen in picture no. 104, which suffered an incendiary bomb attack on 16th April 1941. (D.Cullum)

109. The Down Bickley Loop was realigned in 1959 and direct connections to down main and local lines provided. No. 34085 *501 Squadron* runs onto the latter on 16th May 1959.

Compare this photograph with no. 106 of the same location before the improvements which raised the speed limits. (S.C.Nash)

110. The new Chislehurst Junction Box was built just north of the bridge carrying the former SER route over LCDR lines. Opened on 31st May 1959, it is seen in 1962. It controlled parts of both routes but since 1983 it has only worked the ex-SER section. (J.N.Faulkner)

PETTS WOOD

111. Opened on 9th July 1928, initially there was only one island platform, this being between the local lines. Class E1 4-4-0 no. 1504 enters the down main line platform on 14th January 1932. (H.C.Casserley)

112. King Arthur class no. 770 *Sir Prianius* speeds through with an up Continental express on 14th May 1932, by which time platform canopies had been erected. The surrounding open countryside was soon developed to house season ticket holders. (H.C.Casserley)

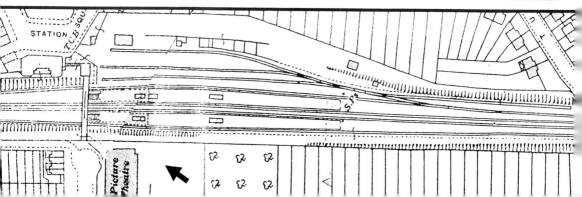

113. Looking towards London on a damp day in April 1963, we can see the extent of the goods yard, which received coal almost ex- clusively. Freight facilities were withdrawn on 7th October 1968. (British Rail)

←

The 1937 survey reveals that semi-detached houses predominated in the development and that a coal yard was provided on the down side.

114. Access to the platforms is via the footbridge (left) which is connected directly to the first floor of the building. (J.Scrace)

ORPINGTON

115. As an up train arrives on 23rd April 1903, we gain a glimpse of the small country station that existed before the 1904 rebuilding, when six platforms were provided. (D.Cullum coll.)

The 1909 map has four sidings to the east and a headshunt to the west of the four tracks from London (left). This is the southern limit of quadruple track. Orpington "A" Box is on the left and "B" is on the right.

→

A 1" to 1 mile scale map from 1910 shows the small town of Orpington, which grew from only 4259 souls in 1901 to 7047 in 1921. The impact of electrification caused a rise to 9870 in the subsequent ten years.

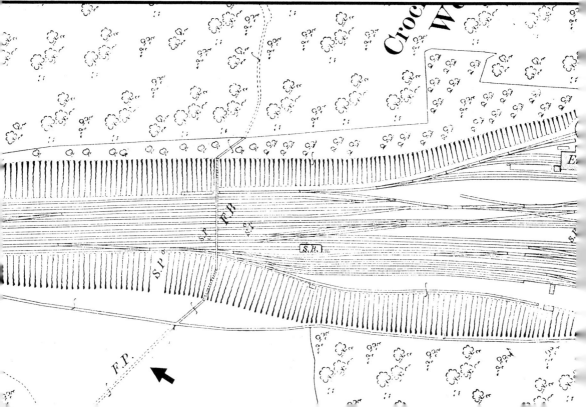

116. Orpington, near the head of the Cray Valley, became the outer limit of suburban train operation, an extensive depot being established here in the early years of this century. This is the southward view in August 1920. The engine shed was still standing in 1991, in use as staff accommodation and offices, as at Littlehampton.
(H.J.Patterson Rutherford)

0049

SOUTHERN RAILWAY.
EAGLE STEAMERS.
DAY EXCURSION
Available as advertised.
Clacton to
ORPINGTON
By G.S.N. Coy's Boat to Tower Pier
thence Via London Bridge

THIRD CLASS

**FOR CONDITIONS
SEE BACK**

SOUTHERN RAILWAY.
EAGLE STEAMERS.
DAY EXCURSION
Available as advertised.
Orpington to
CLACTON
Via London Bridge thence by
G.S.N. Coy's Boat from Tower Pier

THIRD CLASS
0049

0450

SOUTHERN RAILWAY.
PRIVILEGE TICKET.
Available for One Month
Including Day of issue and return.
Issued subject to the conditions
(a) on the Privilege Ticket Order
and (b) on the back thereof.
Woolwich Arsenal to
CHARING CROSS
First Class

SOUTHERN RAILWAY.
PRIVILEGE TICKET.
Available for One Week
Including Day of issue
Charing X.
Woolwich Ar.
Charing Cross to
WOOLWICH ARSENAL
First Class
0450

117. Recorded in May 1948, the scene changed little with the advent of electrification, the carriage shed and washer being the main additions. The 3SUBs have all had a new and wider steel coach inserted, eliminating the pairs of trailer coaches seen earlier. On the right, two sets are berthed on the goods shed road. (British Rail)

118. A new signal box was opened at the London end of platforms 3 and 4 on 4th March 1962, "A" Box (seen in the previous two pictures) and "B" Box (at the south end of the island platform) closing at that time. (J.Scrace)

119. In 1991 the station retained full use of the four through and two bay platforms provided in 1904. Parcel facilities were available but general goods traffic ceased on 7th October 1968. This and the next photograph were taken in September 1990. (J.Scrace)

120. Thameslink services to stations in North London were introduced in May 1988, enhancing the already excellent service to Victoria, Charing Cross and many Kent destinations. In 1991, plans were announced to transfer carriage berthing to Hither Green, to extend the platforms and to make alterations for the Channel Tunnel trains. (J.Scrace)

Easebourne Lane, Midhurst. West Sussex. GU29 9AZ
(0730) 813169
Write or telephone for our latest booklist

BRANCH LINES

BRANCH LINES TO MIDHURST
BRANCH LINES AROUND MIDHURST
BRANCH LINES TO HORSHAM
BRANCH LINE TO SELSEY
BRANCH LINES TO EAST GRINSTEAD
BRANCH LINES TO ALTON
BRANCH LINE TO TENTERDEN
BRANCH LINES TO NEWPORT
BRANCH LINES TO TUNBRIDGE WELLS
BRANCH LINE TO SWANAGE
BRANCH LINE TO LYME REGIS
BRANCH LINE TO FAIRFORD
BRANCH LINE TO ALLHALLOWS
BRANCH LINES AROUND ASCOT
BRANCH LINE AROUND WEYMOUTH
BRANCH LINE TO HAWKHURST
BRANCH LINES AROUND EFFINGHAM JN
BRANCH LINE TO MINEHEAD
BRANCH LINE TO SHREWSBURY
BRANCH LINES AROUND HUNTINGDON
BRANCH LINES TO SEATON AND SIDMOUTH

SOUTH COAST RAILWAYS

CHICHESTER TO PORTSMOUTH
BRIGHTON TO EASTBOURNE
RYDE TO VENTNOR
EASTBOURNE TO HASTINGS
PORTSMOUTH TO SOUTHAMPTON
HASTINGS TO ASHFORD
SOUTHAMPTON TO BOURNEMOUTH
ASHFORD TO DOVER
BOURNEMOUTH TO WEYMOUTH
DOVER TO RAMSGATE

SOUTHERN MAIN LINES

HAYWARDS HEATH TO SEAFORD
EPSOM TO HORSHAM
CRAWLEY TO LITTLEHAMPTON
THREE BRIDGES TO BRIGHTON
WATERLOO TO WOKING
VICTORIA TO EAST CROYDON
EAST CROYDON TO THREE BRIDGES
WOKING TO SOUTHAMPTON
WATERLOO TO WINDSOR
LONDON BRIDGE TO EAST CROYDON
BASINGSTOKE TO SALISBURY
SITTINGBOURNE TO RAMSGATE
YEOVIL TO EXETER

COUNTRY RAILWAY ROUTES

BOURNEMOUTH TO EVERCREECH JN
READING TO GUILDFORD
WOKING TO ALTON
BATH TO EVERCREECH JUNCTION
GUILDFORD TO REDHILL
EAST KENT LIGHT RAILWAY
FAREHAM TO SALISBURY
BURNHAM TO EVERCREECH JUNCTION
REDHILL TO ASHFORD
YEOVIL TO DORCHESTER
ANDOVER TO SOUTHAMPTON

LONDON SUBURBAN RAILWAYS

CHARING CROSS TO DARTFORD
HOLBORN VIADUCT TO LEWISHAM
KINGSTON & HOUNSLOW LOOPS
CRYSTAL PALACE AND CATFORD LOOP
LEWISHAM TO DARTFORD

STEAMING THROUGH

STEAMING THROUGH EAST HANTS
STEAMING THROUGH SURREY
STEAMING THROUGH WEST SUSSEX
STEAMING THROUGH THE ISLE OF WIGHT
STEAMING THROUGH WEST HANTS

OTHER RAILWAY BOOKS

GARRAWAY FATHER & SON
LONDON CHATHAM & DOVER RAILWAY
INDUSTRIAL RAILWAYS OF THE S. EAST
WEST SUSSEX RAILWAYS IN THE 1980s
SOUTH EASTERN RAILWAY

OTHER BOOKS

WALKS IN THE WESTERN HIGH WEALD
TILLINGBOURNE BUS STORY

MILITARY DEFENCE OF WEST SUSSEX
BATTLE OVER SUSSEX 1940

SURREY WATERWAYS
KENT AND EAST SUSSEX WATERWAYS
HAMPSHIRE WATERWAYS